HEREDITY AND THE
AETIOLOGY OF THE NEUROSES

BY

SIGMUND FREUD

British Library Cataloguing-in-Publication Data
A catalogue record for this book is available from the
British Library

Contents

Contents

Sigmund Freud

Sigismund Schlomo Freud was born on 6th May 1856, in the Moravian town of Příbor, now part of the Czech Republic.

Sigmund was the eldest of eight children to Jewish Galician parents, Jacob and Amalia Freud. After Freud's father lost his business as a result of the Panic of 1857, the family were forced to move to Leipzig and then Vienna to avoid poverty. It was in Vienna that the nine-year-old Sigmund enrolled at the Leopoldstädter Kommunal-Realgymnasium before beginning his medical training at the University of Vienna in 1873, at the age of just 17. He studied a variety of subjects, including philosophy, physiology, and zoology, graduating with an MD in 1881.

The following year, Freud began his medical career in Theodor Meynert's psychiatric clinic at the Vienna General Hospital. He worked there until 1886 when he set up in private practice and began specialising in "nervous disorders". In the same year he married Merth Bernays, with whom he had 6 children between 1887 and 1895.

In the period between 1896 and 1901, Freud isolated himself from his colleagues and began work on developing the basics of his psychoanalytic theory. He published *The Interpretation of Dreams*, in 1899, to a lacklustre reception, but continued to produce works such as *The Psychopathology of Everyday Life* (1901) and *Three Essays on the Theory of Sexuality* (1905). He held a weekly meeting at his home known as the "Wednesday Psychological Society" which eventually developed into the Vienna Psycho-Analytic Society. His ideas gained momentum and by the end of the decade his methods were being used internationally by neurologists and psychiatrists.

Freud made a huge and lasting contribution to the field of psychology with many of his methods still being used in modern psychoanalysis. He inspired much discussion on the wealth of theories he produced and the reactions to his works began a century of great psychological investigation.

In 1930 Freud fled Vienna due to rise of Nazism and resided in England until his death from mouth cancer on 23rd September 1939.

HEREDITY AND THE AETIOLOGY OF THE NEUROSES
(1896A)

I am addressing in particular the disciples of J.-M. Charcot, in order to put forward some objections to the aetiological theory of the neuroses which was handed on to us by our teacher.

The role attributed in that theory to nervous heredity is well known: it is the sole true and indispensable cause of neurotic affections, and the other aetiological influences can aspire only to the name of *agents provocateurs*. Such was the opinion laid down by the great man himself and by his pupils, M M. Guinon, Gilles de la Tourette, Janet and others, in regard to the major neurosis, hysteria; and I believe the same view is held in France and in most other places in regard to the other neuroses, though, where these states analogous to hysteria are concerned, it has not been promulgated in so solemn and decided a manner.

I have long entertained doubts on this subject, but I have had to wait to find corroborative facts in my daily experience as a doctor. My objections are now of a double order: factual arguments and arguments derived from speculation. I will begin with the former, arranging them according to the importance I ascribe to them.

I

(*a*) Affections which are fairly often remote from the domain of neuropathology, and which do not necessarily depend on a disease of the nervous system, have sometimes been regarded as nervous and as showing the presence of a hereditary neuropathic tendency. This has been so with true facial neuralgias and with many headaches which were thought to be nervous but which arose rather from post-infectious pathological changes and suppuration in the pharyngo-nasal cavities. I feel convinced that the patients would benefit if we were more often to hand over the treatment of these affections to the rhinological surgeons.

(*b*) All the nervous affections found in a patient's family, without consideration of their frequence or severity, have been accepted as a basis for charging him with a hereditary nervous taint. Does not this way of looking at things imply drawing a sharp line between families which are clear of all nervous predisposition and families which are subject to them to an unlimited extent? And do not the facts argue in favour of the contrary view that there are transitions and degrees in nervous disposition and that no family escapes it altogether?

(*c*) Our opinion of the aetiological role of heredity in nervous illnesses ought decidedly to be based on an impartial statistical examination and not on a *petitio principi*. Until such an examination has been made we ought to believe that the existence of acquired nervous disorders is just as possible as that of hereditary ones. But if there can be nervous disorders that are acquired by people without a predisposition, it can no longer be denied that the nervous affections met with in our patient's relatives may partly have arisen in that way. It will then no longer be possible to quote them as conclusive evidence of the hereditary disposition imputed to the patient by reason of his family history, for a retrospective diagnosis of the illnesses of ancestors or absent members of a family can only very rarely be successfully made.

(*d*) Those who are adherents of M. Fournier and M. Erb in the matter of the part played by syphilis in the aetiology of tabes dorsalis and progressive paralysis have learned that powerful aetiological influences must be recognized whose collaboration is indispensable for the pathogenesis of certain illnesses which could not be produced by heredity alone. Nevertheless M. Charcot remained to the very last (as I know from a private letter I had from him) strictly opposed to Fournier's theory, which is, however, gaining ground every day.

(*e*) There is no doubt that certain nervous disorders can develop in people who are perfectly healthy and whose family is above reproach. This is a matter of daily observation in cases of Beard's neurasthenia; if neurasthenia were restricted to people who were predisposed, it would never have attained the importance and extent with which we are familiar.

(*f*) In nervous pathology there is *similar heredity* and what is known as *dissimilar heredity*. No objection can be made to the former; it is in fact a very remarkable thing that in the disorders which depend on similar heredity (Thomsen's disease, Friedreich's disease, the myopathies, Huntington's chorea, etc.) we never come across a trace of any other accessory aetiological influence. But dissimilar heredity, which is much more important than the other, leaves gaps which would have to be filled before a satisfactory solution of aetiological problems could be reached. Dissimilar heredity consists in the fact that the members of the same family are found to be affected by the most various nervous disorders, functional and organic, without its being possible to discover any law determining the replacement of one illness by another or the order of their succession through the generations. Alongside of the sick members of these families there are others who remain healthy; and the theory of dissimilar heredity does not tell us why one person tolerates the same hereditary load without succumbing to it or why another person, who is sick, should choose this particular nervous affection from among all the illnesses which make up the great family of nervous diseases instead of choosing another one - hysteria instead of epilepsy or insanity, and so on. Since there is no such thing as chance in neurotic pathogenesis any more than anywhere else, it must be allowed that it is not heredity that presides over the choice of the particular nervous disorder which is to develop in the predisposed member of a family, but that there are grounds for suspecting the existence of other aetiological influences, of a less incomprehensible nature, which would then deserve to be called the *specific aetiology* of such and such a nervous affection. Without the existence of this special aetiological factor, heredity could have done nothing; it would have lent itself to the production of another nervous disorder if the specific aetiology in question had been replaced by some other influence.

II

There has been too little research into these specific and determining causes of nervous disorders, for the attention of physicians has remained dazzled by the grandiose prospect of the aetiological precondition of heredity. Those causes nevertheless deserve to be made the object of industrious study. Although their pathogenic power is in general only accessory to that of heredity, great practical interest attaches to the knowledge of this specific aetiology; it will allow our therapeutic efforts a path of access, whereas hereditary disposition, which is something fixed in advance for the patient from his birth, brings our efforts to a halt with its unapproachable power.

I have been engaged for years in researches into the aetiology of the major neuroses (functional nervous states analogous to hysteria) and it is the result of those studies that I propose to describe to you in the following pages. To avoid any possible misunderstanding I shall begin by making two remarks on the nosography of the neuroses and on the aetiology of the neuroses in general.

I was obliged to begin my work with a nosographic innovation. I found reason to set alongside of hysteria the obsessional neurosis (*Zwangsneurose*) as a self-sufficient and independent disorder, although the majority of the authorities place obsessions among the syndromes constituting mental degeneracy or confuse them with neurasthenia. I for my part, by examining the psychical mechanism of obsessions, had learnt that they are connected with hysteria more closely than one might suppose.

Hysteria and obsessional neurosis form the first group of the major neuroses studied by me. The second contains Beard's neurasthenia, which I have divided up into two functional states separated by their aetiology as well as by their symptomatic appearance - *neurasthenia* proper and the *anxiety neurosis* (*Angstneurose*), a name which, I may say in passing, I am not pleased with myself. I gave my detailed reasons for making this separation, which I consider necessary, in a paper published in 1895.

As regards the aetiology of the neuroses, I think it should be recognized in theory that aetiological influences, differing among themselves in their importance and in the manner in which they are related to the effect they produce, can be grouped in three classes: (1) *Preconditions*, which are indispensable for producing the disorder concerned but which are of a general nature and are equally met with in the aetiology of many other disorders; (2) *Concurrent Causes*, which share the character of preconditions in that they function in the causation of other disorders as well as in that of the disorder under consideration, but which are not indispensable for the production of the latter; and (3) *Specific*

Causes, which are as indispensable as the preconditions, but are of a limited nature and appear only in the aetiology of the disorder for which they are specific.

In the pathogenesis of the major neuroses, then, heredity fulfils the role of a *precondition*, powerful in every case and even indispensable in most cases. It could not do without the collaboration of the specific causes; but the importance of hereditary disposition is proved by the fact that the same specific causes acting on a healthy individual produce no manifest pathological effect, whereas in a predisposed person their action causes the neurosis to come to light, whose development will be proportionate in intensity and extent to the degree of the hereditary precondition.

Thus the action of heredity is comparable to that of a multiplier in an electric circuit, which exaggerates the visible deviation of the needle, but which cannot determine its direction.

There is yet another thing to be noted in the relations between the hereditary precondition and the specific causes of neuroses. Experience shows - what one might have guessed in advance - that in these questions of aetiology one should not neglect the relative quantities, so to speak, of the aetiological influences. But one could not have guessed the following fact, which seems to arise from my observations: namely that heredity and the specific causes can replace each other as regards quantity, that the same pathological effect will be produced by the coincidence of a very serious specific aetiology with a moderate disposition or of a severely loaded nervous heredity with a slight specific influence. And we shall simply be meeting not unexpected extreme instances in this series if we come upon cases of neurosis in which we shall look in vain for an appreciable degree of hereditary disposition, provided that what is lacking is made up for by a powerful specific influence.

As *concurrent* (or auxiliary) *causes* of neuroses may be enumerated all the stock agents met with elsewhere: emotional disturbance, physical exhaustion, acute illnesses, intoxications, traumatic accidents, intellectual overwork, etc. I maintain that none of these, not even the last, enters into the aetiology of the neuroses regularly or necessarily, and I am aware that to declare this opinion is to put oneself in direct opposition to a theory which is looked upon as universally accepted and irreproachable. Since Beard declared that neurasthenia was the fruit of our modern civilization, he has only met with believers; but I find it impossible to accept this view. A laborious study of the neuroses has taught me that the specific aetiology of the neuroses has escaped Beard's notice.

I have no desire to depreciate the aetiological importance of these stock agents. Since they are very various, occur very frequently and are most often named by patients themselves, they become more prominent than the specific causes of the neuroses - an aetiology which is either hidden or unknown. Fairly frequently they fulfil the function of *agents provocateurs* which render manifest a neurosis that has previously been latent; and a practical interest attaches to them, for a consideration of these stock causes may offer lines of approach to a therapy which does not aim at a radical cure and is content with repressing the illness to its former state of latency.

But it is not possible to establish any constant and close relation between one of these stock causes and one or other form of nervous affection. Emotional disturbance, for instance, is found equally in the aetiology of hysteria, obsessions and neurasthenia, as well as in that of epilepsy, Parkinson's disease, diabetes and many others.

Stock concurrent causes can replace the specific aetiology in respect of quantity, but can never take its place entirely. There are numerous cases in which all the aetiological influences are represented by the hereditary precondition and the specific cause, stock causes being absent. In the other cases indispensable aetiological factors are not in themselves sufficient in quantity to bring about an outbreak of neurosis; a state of apparent health may be maintained for a long time, though it is in reality a state of predisposition to neurosis. It is then enough for a stock cause to come into action as well, and the neurosis becomes manifest. But it must be clearly pointed out that under these conditions the nature of the stock cause which supervenes is a matter of complete indifference - whether it is an emotion, a trauma, an infectious illness or anything else. The pathological effect will not be modified according to this variation; the nature of the neurosis will always be dominated by the pre-existing specific cause.

What, then are the specific causes of neuroses? Is there a single one or are there several? And is it possible to establish a constant aetiological relation between a particular cause and a particular neurotic effect, in such a way that each of the major neuroses can be attributed to a special aetiology?

On the basis of a laborious examination of the facts, I shall maintain that this last supposition is quite in agreement with reality, that each of the major neuroses which I have enumerated has as its immediate cause one particular disturbance of the economics of the nervous system, and that these functional pathological modifications *have as their common source the subject's sexual life, whether they lie in a disorder of his contemporary sexual life or in important events in his past life.*

This, to tell the truth, is no new, unheard-of proposition. Sexual disorders have always been admitted among the causes of nervous illness, but they have been subordinated to heredity - and co-ordinated with the other *agents provocateurs*; their aetiological influence has been restricted to a limited number of observed cases. Physicians had even fallen into the habit of not investigating them unless the patient brought them up himself. What gives its distinctive character to my line of approach is that I elevate these sexual influences to the rank of specific causes, that I recognize their action in every case of neurosis, and finally that I trace a regular parallelism, a proof of a special aetiological relation between the nature of the sexual influence and the pathological species of the neurosis.

I am quite sure that this theory will call up a storm of contradictions from contemporary physicians. But this is not the place in which to present the documents and the experiences which have forced me to my convictions, nor to explain the true meaning of the rather vague expression 'disorders of the economics of the nervous system'. This will be done, most fully, I hope, in a work on the subject which I have in preparation. In the present paper I limit myself to reporting my findings.

Neurasthenia proper, if we detach anxiety neurosis from it, has a very monotonous clinical appearance: fatigue, intracranial pressure, flatulent dyspepsia, constipation, spinal paraesthesias, sexual weakness, etc. The only specific aetiology it allows of is (immoderate) masturbation or spontaneous emissions.

It is the prolonged and intense action of this pernicious sexual satisfaction which is enough on its own account to provoke a neurasthenic neurosis or which imposes on the subject the special neurasthenic stamp that is manifested later under the influence of an incidental accessory cause. I have also come across people presenting the indications of a neurasthenic constitution in whom I have not succeeded in bringing to light the aetiology I have mentioned; but I have at least shown that the sexual function has never developed to its normal level in these patients; they seemed to have been endowed by heredity with a sexual constitution analogous to what is brought about in a neurasthenic as a result of masturbation.

The anxiety neurosis exhibits a much richer clinical picture: irritability, states of anxious expectation, phobias, anxiety attacks, complete or rudimentary, attacks of fear and of vertigo, tremors, sweating, congestion, dyspnoea, tachycardia, etc., chronic diarrhoea, chronic locomotor vertigo, hyperaesthesia, insomnia, etc.[1] It is easily revealed as being the specific effect of various disorders of sexual life which possess a characteristic common to all of them. Enforced abstinence, unconsummated genital excitation (excitation which is not relieved by a sexual act), coition which is imperfect or interrupted (which does not end in gratification), sexual efforts which exceed the subject's psychical capacity, etc. - all these agents, which occur only too frequently in modern life, seem to agree in the fact that they disturb the equilibrium of the psychical and somatic functions in sexual acts, and that they prevent the psychical participation necessary in order to free the nervous economy from sexual tension.

¹ For the symptomatology as well as for the aetiology of anxiety neurosis, see my paper referred to above.

These remarks, which perhaps contain the germ of a theoretical explanation of the functional mechanism of the neurosis in question, give rise already to a suspicion that a complete and truly scientific exposition of the subject is not possible at the present time, and that it would be necessary to start off by approaching the physiological problem of sexual life from a fresh angle.

I will say finally that the pathogenesis of neurasthenia and anxiety neurosis can easily do without the co-operation of a hereditary disposition. That is the outcome of daily observation. But if heredity is present, the development of the neurosis will be affected by its powerful influence.

As regards the second class of major neuroses, hysteria and obsessional neurosis, the solution of the aetiological problem is of surprising simplicity and uniformity. I owe my results to a new method of psycho-analysis, Josef Breuer's exploratory procedure; it is a little intricate, but it is irreplaceable, so fertile has it shown itself to be in throwing light upon the obscure paths of unconscious ideation. By means of that procedure - this is not the place in which to describe it ¹ - hysterical symptoms are traced back to their origin, which is always found in some event of the subject's sexual life appropriate for the production of a distressing emotion. Travelling backwards into the patient's past, step by step, and always guided by the organic train of symptoms and of memories and thoughts aroused, I finally reached the starting-point of the pathological process; and I was obliged to see that at bottom the same thing was present in all the cases submitted to analysis - the action of an agent which must be accepted as the specific cause of hysteria.

[1] See *Studies on Hysteria*, by Breuer and Freud, 1895.

This agent is indeed a memory relating to sexual life; but it is one which presents two characteristics of the first importance. The event of which the subject has retained an unconscious memory is *a precocious experience of sexual relations with actual excitement of the genitals, resulting from sexual abuse committed by another person*; and *the period of life* at which this fatal event takes place is *earliest youth - the years up to the age of eight to ten, before the child has reached sexual maturity.

A passive sexual experience before puberty: this, then, is the specific aetiology of hysteria.

I will without delay add some factual details and some commentary to the result I have announced, in order to combat the scepticism with which I expect to meet. I have been able to carry out a complete psycho-analysis in thirteen cases of hysteria, three of that number being true combinations of hysteria and obsessional neurosis. (I do not speak of hysteria *with* obsessions.) In none of these cases was an event of the kind defined above missing. It was represented either by a brutal assault committed by an adult or by a seduction less rapid and less repulsive, but reaching the same conclusion. In seven out of the thirteen cases the intercourse was between children on both sides - sexual relations between a little girl and a boy a little older (most often her brother) who had himself been the victim of an earlier seduction. These relations sometimes continued for years, until the little guilty parties reached puberty; the boy would repeat the same practices with the little girl over and over again and without alteration - practices to which he himself had been subjected by some female servant or governess and which on account of their origin were often of a disgusting sort. In a few cases there was a combination of an assault and relations between children or a repetition of a brutal abuse.

The date of this precocious experience varied. In two cases the series started in the little creature's second year (?); the commonest age in my observations is the fourth or fifth year. It may be somewhat by accident, but I have formed an impression from this that a passive sexual experience occurring only after the age of from eight to ten is no longer able to serve as the foundation of the neurosis.

How is it possible to remain convinced of the reality of these analytic confessions which claim to be memories preserved from the earliest childhood? and how is one to arm oneself against the tendency to lies and the facility of invention which are attributed to hysterical subjects? I should accuse myself of blame-worthy credulity if I did not possess more conclusive evidence. But the fact is that these patients never repeat these stories spontaneously, nor do they ever in the course of a treatment suddenly present the physician with the complete recollection of a scene of this kind. One only succeeds in awakening the psychical trace of a precocious sexual event under the most energetic pressure of the analytic procedure, and against an enormous resistance. Moreover, the memory must be extracted from them piece by piece, and while it is being awakened in their consciousness they become the prey to an emotion which it would be hard to counterfeit.

Conviction will follow in the end, if one is not influenced by the patients' behaviour, provided that one can follow in detail the report of a psycho-analysis of a case of hysteria.

The precocious event has left an indelible imprint on the history of the case; it is represented in it by a host of symptoms and of special features which could be accounted for in no other way; it is peremptorily called for by the subtle but solid interconnections of the intrinsic structure of the neurosis; the therapeutic effect of the analysis lags behind if one has not penetrated so far; and one is then left with no choice but to reject or to believe the whole.

Is it understandable that a precocious sexual experience of this kind, undergone by an individual whose sex is barely differentiated, can become the source of a persistent psychical abnormality like hysteria? And how would this supposition fit in with our present ideas on the psychical mechanism of that neurosis? A satisfactory reply can be given to the first of these questions. It is precisely because the subject is in his infancy that the precocious sexual excitation produces little or no effect at the time; but its psychical trace is preserved. Later, when at puberty the reactions of the sexual organs have developed to a level incommensurable with their infantile condition, it comes about in one way or another that this unconscious psychical trace is awakened. Thanks to the change due to puberty, the memory will display a power which was completely lacking from the event itself. *The memory will operate as though it were a contemporary event.* What happens is, as it were, *a posthumous action by a sexual trauma.*

So far as I can see, this awakening of a sexual memory after puberty, when the event itself has happened at a time long before that period, forms the only psychological instance of the effect of a *memory* surpassing that of an actual event. But the constellation is an abnormal one, which touches a weak side of the psychical mechanism and is bound to produce a pathological psychical effect.

I believe I can see that *this inverse relation between the psychical effect of the memory and of the event* contains the reason for *the memory remaining unconscious.*

In this way we arrive at a very complex psychical problem, but one which, properly appreciated, promises to throw a vivid light on the most delicate questions of psychical life.

The ideas put forward here, which have as their starting point the finding of psycho-analysis to the effect that a memory of a precocious sexual experience is always found as the specific cause of hysteria, are not in harmony with the psychological theory of neuroses held by M. Janet, nor with any other; but they agree perfectly with my own speculations on the *'Abwehrneurosen'*, as I have developed them elsewhere.

All the events subsequent to puberty to which an influence must be attributed upon the development of the hysterical neurosis and upon the formation of its symptoms are in fact only concurrent causes - *'agents provocateurs'* as Charcot used to say, although for him nervous heredity occupied the place which I claim for the precocious sexual experience. These accessory agents are not subject to the strict conditions imposed on the specific causes; analysis demonstrates in an irrefutable fashion that they enjoy a pathogenic influence for hysteria only owing to their faculty for awakening the unconscious psychical trace of the childhood event. It is also thanks to their connection with the primary pathogenic impression, and inspired by it, that their memories will become unconscious in their turn and will be able to assist in the growth of a psychical activity withdrawn from the power of the conscious functions.

The obsessional neurosis (*Zwangsneurose*) arises from a specific cause very analogous to that of hysteria. Here too we find a precocious sexual event, occurring before puberty, the memory of which becomes active during or after that period; and the same remarks and arguments which I put forward in connection with hysteria will apply to my observations of the other neurosis (six cases, three of which were pure ones). There is only one difference which seems capital. At the basis of the aetiology of hysteria we found an event of passive sexuality, an experience submitted to with indifference or with a small degree of annoyance or fright. In obsessional neurosis it is a question on the other hand, of an event which has given *pleasure*, of an act of aggression inspired by desire (in the case of a boy) or of a participation in sexual relations accompanied by enjoyment (in the case of a little girl). The obsessional ideas, when their intimate meaning has been recognized by analysis, when they have been reduced, as it were, to their simplest expression, are nothing other than *reproaches addressed by the subject himself on account of this anticipated sexual enjoyment,* but reproaches distorted by an unconscious psychical work of transformation and substitution.

The very fact of sexual aggressions of this kind taking place at such a tender age seems to reveal the influence of a previous seduction of which the precocity of sexual desire would be the consequence. In the cases analysed by me analysis confirms this suspicion. In this way an interesting fact is explained which is always found in these cases of obsessions: the regular complication of the framework of symptoms by a certain number of symptoms which are simply hysterical.

The importance of the active element in sexual life as a cause of obsessions, and of sexual passivity for the pathogenesis of hysteria, even seems to unveil the reason for the more intimate connection of hysteria with the female sex and the preference of men for obsessional neurosis. One sometimes comes across a pair of neurotic patients who were a pair of little lovers in their earliest childhood - the man suffering from obsessions and the woman from hysteria. If they are a brother and sister, one might mistake for a result of nervous heredity what is in fact the consequence of precocious sexual experiences.

There are no doubt pure and isolated cases of hysteria or obsessions, independent of neurasthenia or anxiety neurosis; but this is not the rule. A psychoneurosis appears more often as an accessory to a neurasthenic neurosis, provoked by it and following its decline. This is because the specific causes of the latter, the contemporary disorders of sexual life, operate at the same time as auxiliary causes of the psychoneuroses, whose specific cause, the memory of the precocious sexual experience, they awaken and revive.

As regards nervous heredity, I am far from being able to estimate correctly its influence in the aetiology of the psychoneuroses. I admit that its presence is indispensable for severe cases; I doubt if it is necessary for slight ones; but I am convinced that nervous heredity by itself is unable to produce psychoneuroses if their specific aetiology, precocious sexual excitation, is missing. I even believe that the decision as to which of the neuroses, hysteria or obsessions, will develop in a given case, is not decided by heredity but a special characteristic of the sexual event in earliest childhood.